Summer

Would You Rather

Game Book

Jesse B. Johnson

www.CrimsonHillBooks.com

Cataloguing in Publication Data

Johnson, Jesse B.

Summer Would You Rather Game Book

Description: Crimson Hill Books trade paperback edition | Nova Scotia, Canada

ISBN:	978-1-990887-89-5 (Paperback – Ingram)
BISAC:	JNF028020 Juvenile Nonfiction: Humor - Jokes & Riddles JNF021050 Juvenile Nonfiction: Games & Activities - Questions & Answers JNF021070 Juvenile Nonfiction: Games & Activities - Word Games
THEMA:	Y - Children's - Teenage & Educational YPC - Children's - Educational: Language, literature & literacy YNU - Children's / Teenage General Interest: Humour & jokes

Record available at https://www.bac-lac.gc.ca/eng/Pages/home.aspx

Book design: Jesse Johnson

Crimson Hill Books
(a division of)
Crimson Hill Products Inc.
Lawrencetown, Nova Scotia
Canada

Crimson Hill
Books

What would YOU rather do?

You could use the questions in this book to spur your imagination. Or for more ideas for your summer activities and fun. Or even to give you some questions to answer in a journal or just to think about.

Summer Would You Rather Game Book also works as a game. You can play it anytime, anywhere. All you need is two or more players. The rules are simple:

The player who takes the first turn chooses one question from this book to answer and answers it. Then they choose a question for the next player to answer.

Every question begins with "Would you rather...?"

There are two choices given to answer. Players must choose one or the other and tell why they are making their choice.

The first player who simply can't make a choice or can't answer is out of the game. The last player left is the winner.

❖ Go tubing with friends? You'd spend all afternoon lounging on truck innertubes, floating down a lazy river.
OR
Go white-water rafting for 3 hours with friends? You'd bounce through rapids on a fast river and might even fall overboard!

❖ Have a family campfire on the beach?
OR
A backyard barbeque?

❖ Go fossil hunting on the East Coast?
OR
On a cross-country treasure hunt?

❖ Learn to scuba dive?
OR
Learn how to rappel down a rock cliff?

❖ Join a water ballet team?
OR
A diving team?

❖ Climb to the top of a giant redwood tree?
OR
Hike to the bottom of Grand Canyon and back?

❖ Swim in the ocean?
OR
Swim in a backyard pool?

❖ Go to school all summer, but then get all of December, January and February as vacation?
OR
Keep the school year exactly the same as now?

❖ Fill up on hot dogs at your family campfire or backyard barbeque?
OR
Hamburgers?

❖ Visit your favorite relatives?
OR
Visit a friend who has moved away?

❖ Go to summer camp on an island in Minnesota?
OR
Go to summer camp in South Carolina?

❖ Learn how to operate a powerboat?
OR
A jet ski?

❖ Dive off of rocks into a northern lake?
OR
A pool on a cruise ship?

❖ Always work every day of the week, but only for 5 hours each day?
OR
Only work on 4 days of the week, but your working days are 10 hours?

❖ Learn what it's like to be an airline pilot?
OR
A helicopter pilot?

❖ Go camping in a tent in your own backyard?
OR
In a national park in a different part of the country?

❖ Earn a swimming certificate?
OR
Teach others how to swim?

❖ Learn how to make ice cream?
OR
Learn how to make 5 different kinds of s'mores?

❖ Help plant a flower garden and look after it?
OR
A vegetable garden?

❖ Read 40 short books this summer?
OR
Read 15 long books this summer?

❖ Trade families with your best friend?
OR
Your family trades homes with their family?

❖ Move somewhere with your family? Where to?
OR
Live exactly where you live now for 10 more years?

❖ Read a fiction book next? (Fiction books tell stories).
OR
A non-fiction book? (Non-fiction books give information).

❖ Adopt a pet dog?
OR
A pet cat?

❖ Meet friends for a badminton game?
OR
Racquetball?

❖ Learn how to knit?
OR
Crochet?

❖ Live where there are four distinct seasons?
OR
Where the weather is always pretty much the same year-round?

❖ Have just a few really close friends?
OR
Know lots of people, but none of them are close friends?

❖ Go on a lazy beach vacation?
OR
An action-packed city vacation?

❖ Help plant a garden for the Food Bank?
OR
Help plant a flower garden to brighten up your neighborhood?

❖ Be a lifeguard at the community pool?
OR
A summer nanny, looking after and entertaining 3 children?

❖ Listen to music?
OR
Dance to music?

❖ Create music by writing it?
OR
Playing it?

❖ Read a good story?
OR
Tell a good story?

❖ Get 1 BIG wish or dream-come-true?
OR
3 smaller wishes?

❖ Take a trip to find all the 'secret' waterfalls in your state or region?
OR
Take a trip to find the best of your favorite summer food in your state or region?

❖ Wake up tomorrow to find out you're a very successful movie star?
OR
Pop singer?

❖ Visit the coldest place on earth?
OR
The hottest?

❖ Go for day-long hikes?
OR
On a hiking vacation where you camp out every night in a tent?

❖ Go hang-gliding?
OR
For a hot-air balloon ride?

❖ Learn how to sew?
OR
How to cook 5 dinners you and your family like, from scratch?

❖ Learn how to surf?
OR
Water-ski?

❖ Learn how to do a backflip dive?
Or
How to hold your breath underwater for as long as you want?

❖ Go whale-watching?
OR
On a hike to spot bald eagles?

❖ Write a play?
OR
Be one of the actors in a play?

❖ Invent a new cookie recipe?
OR
A new topping for popcorn?

❖ Take a road trip vacation? To where?
OR
Fly somewhere for your vacation? Where?

❖ Have your favorite pop star or rock star ask you to help them write a song for their next album?
OR
Work with your favorite rap singer on their next album?

❖ Go to a baseball game?
OR
Be one of the players for that game?

❖ Learn a new language this summer by taking classroom lessons?
OR
During an immersion vacation where the language you're learning is the only one spoken?

❖ Have a part-time job this summer? What job?
OR
Not? Why?

❖ Paint a fence?
OR
Sand and paint a sailboat's hull?

❖ Take a 'trip of a lifetime' to anywhere you want to go, with anyone you want to go with, just once in your life?
OR
Always take smaller, shorter trips, but you can go somewhere once a year?

❖ Take sailing lessons?
OR
Sailboard lessons?

❖ Live all summer in a luxury yurt near the seaside?
OR
In an old hunter's cabin in the mountains?

❖ Turn off your computer for one week?
OR
Turn off your TV for one week?

❖ Go birdwatching for a weekend with a friend?
OR
Wilderness hiking, hoping to spot wild animals like bears or wolves?

❖ Visit New York City?
OR
Los Angeles?

❖ Visit Chicago?
OR
Seattle?

❖ Take basic cooking lessons?
OR
Baking lessons?

❖ Adopt a pet snake?
OR
A pet pygmy pig?

❖ Share your vacation with a complete stranger?
OR
With someone you've known since Grade 2?

❖ Let AI choose your next vacation destination?
OR
Let your family choose where you'll go next?

❖ A paint-ball battle with all your friends?
OR
A water-gun battle?

❖ Enter a hot pepper-eating contest?
OR
A frozen slushie eating contest?

❖ A sailing yacht vacation in the Caribbean?
OR
A small ship cruise from Boston to Montreal?

❖ Go to any summer camp you choose for 2 weeks?
OR
Go with your family to Disneyland?

❖ Play frisbee fetch with a happy dog?
OR
Frisbee golf with your best friend?

❖ Have smoothies for dinner?
OR
Pizza for breakfast?

❖ Act as a paid extra in a movie being made in your town?
OR
Just watch some of the scenes being filmed from the sidelines?

❖ Get an autograph from your favorite player after a pro ballgame?
OR
Catch the game-winner ball?

❖ Go to circus school for 3 weeks this summer?
OR
Go to falconry school and learn how to work with raptors?

❖ Make a movie with your friends?
OR
Put on a play?

❖ Make 3 new friends this summer?
OR
Spend lots of time hanging out with your 3 best friends?

❖ Suddenly find out you can fly?
OR
You can run faster than anyone you know?

❖ Help paint a mural on a wall in your town or city?
OR
Help tidy up a spare lot to make it a community park?

❖ Use your vacation time this summer to start a side-gig business?
OR
Work through a list of home fix-up tasks during your vacation?

❖ Live on a houseboat this summer?
OR
Live in a lighthouse?

❖ Spend summer perfecting your skateboard tricks?
OR
Learning how to play the tuba?

❖ Help a famous game designer create their next game?
OR
Meet a famous competition gamer and learn how they do it?

❖ Go to a stadium rock concert?
OR
A smaller outdoor concert?

❖ Ride a giant rollercoaster 3 times?
OR
Go down a giant waterslide as many times as you want?

❖ Enter a sandcastle-building competition?
OR
A chainsaw sculpture contest?

❖ Visit a science museum?
OR
An art museum?

❖ Be immune to mosquito bites?
OR
Sunburn?

❖ Volunteer to read to adults with low vision or who are blind?
OR
Volunteer to teach little children how to read?

❖ Be able to go for a swim any time you feel like it?
OR
Be able to go for a country walk anytime?

❖ Take a ride on a steam train?
OR
A carriage ride city tour?

❖ Be a helper at your local library?
OR
A hospital volunteer, working in the gift shop or the cafeteria?

❖ Buy a home that is small but already updated and ready to move in to?
OR
Buy a former warehouse that has lots of space, but it needs work and you'll have to do most of it yourself?

❖ Take a ride with a jetpack?
OR
Go to astronaut school for 1 week?

❖ Go for a farm-stay vacation?
OR
Live at an art colony for a month?

❖ Catch fireflies?
OR
Minnows?

❖ Eat a 15-course dinner at a Michelin-starred restaurant for a special occasion this summer?
OR
Eat out at fast-food restaurants all summer as often as you want?

❖ Work at a job you dislike intensely, but it's making you rich?
OR
Work at your passion project full time, but you earn very little money and have to live very modestly?

❖ Have a sauna in your home?
OR
A giant whirlpool bathtub?

❖ Get around in a golf cart?
OR
On an electric bicycle?

❖ Try out parkour, also called PK?
OR
Flag football?

❖ Go to see a cricket match?
OR
A lacrosse match?

❖ Join a squash team?
OR
A lacrosse team?

❖ Own a new half-ton truck?
 OR
 A vintage sports car?

❖ Have a beach party with your family?
 OR
 Go to an outdoor concert?

❖ Watch a fireworks show?
 OR
 A parade?

❖ Toast marshmallows over a campfire?
 OR
 Hotdogs?

❖ Get an ice cream cone right now?
 OR
 Cake?

❖ Go to a giant amusement park?
 OR
 A museum?

❖ Play in an arcade all afternoon?
 OR
 Go to a board games event?

❖ Go to science camp for 1 week?
 OR
 Computer camp?

❖ Dig for worms so you can go fishing?
OR
Go digging on the beach for clams or scallops for your dinner?

❖ Go to music camp for 1 week?
OR
Sports camp? Which sport?

❖ Perform at an aquarium as a mermaid?
OR
Be an animal caregiver at the aquarium?

❖ Get an ant farm?
OR
25 houseplants?

❖ Live alone on a deserted island for a month before you are rescued?
OR
Find yourself on that island and you aren't alone. Also stranded there are 3 people you don't really like.

❖ Get up early to see the sunrise?
OR
Pause in the evening to watch the sunset?

❖ Swim under a waterfall?
OR
Walk along the path behind the waterfall?

❖ Take a ride on the London Eye in England?
OR
The Orlando Eye, in Florida?

❖ Prepare to compete in skateboarding at the 2028 Olympics?
OR
Breakdancing?

❖ Go to an aquarium to see many freshwater and ocean fish and animals?
OR
Go to a planetarium to see a show featuring stars and planets?

❖ Lie on your back and watch cloud shapes drifting by, making up stories about them?
OR
Watch the stars come out, looking for the constellations and telling stories about them?

❖ Have a lot of free time this summer to do anything you feel like doing?
OR
Have a lot of scheduled activities this summer, getting to try out lots of different things?

❖ Walk barefoot on hot sand once because you lost your flip-flops?
OR
Have to wear flip-flops all the time for a month?

❖ Search for a 4-leaf clover?
   OR
   Sea glass on the beach?

❖ Run through a sprinkler?
   OR
   Soak your feet in a kiddie pool?

❖ Own an all-terrain vehicle (ATV)?
   OR
   A hoverboard?

❖ Plan a surprise party for your best friend?
   OR
   Someone gives you a surprise party?

❖ Meet your favorite actor?
   OR
   Meet a famous person you admire? Who are they?

❖ Take tap-dancing lessons?
   OR
   Break-dancing lessons?

❖ Join a water polo team?
   OR
   Play polo on horseback?

❖ Learn how to bake a pie?
   OR
   Make a cake?

❖ Build a dollhouse?
OR
Make all the furniture and everything else in the dollhouse?

❖ Get a part-time job at a flower farm?
OR
A garden center?

❖ Take lessons in oil painting?
OR
Watercolor painting?

❖ Go to art camp?
OR
Acting camp?

❖ Be a model in a fashion show?
OR
Design 5 outfits for models to wear in the fashion show?

❖ Earn spending money with your own lawncare business?
OR
As a dog-walker?

❖ Your family buys a family car that runs on electricity?
OR
A sports car that runs on gasoline?

❖ Be the oldest person in your friend group?
OR
The youngest?

❖ Be the tallest person in your family?
OR
The shortest?

❖ Go fishing off a dock or pier?
OR
On the ocean?

❖ Go swimming?
OR
Just lie on the beach and read or take a nap?

❖ Go roller skating?
OR
Bowling?

❖ Eat lobster at a shore dinner?
OR
Steak at a backyard barbeque?

❖ Spend the afternoon at a movie theater?
OR
Go-cart track?

❖ Own a canoe?
OR
A kayak?

❖ Own a motorboat?
   OR
   A sailboat?

❖ Own a rowboat?
   OR
   A paddleboat?

❖ Go on a day-long horseback trail ride?
   OR
   For a day-long hike through the forest?

❖ Scrub all the walls clean in your home?
   OR
   Paint them?

❖ Learn advanced computer coding this summer?
   OR
   How to predict the weather accurately?

❖ Help build a backyard deck?
   OR
   A garden shed?

❖ Write a song, record it and put it up on YouTube?
   OR
   Sell jewelry you make on Etsy?

❖ Sell your art or a craft you make at a craft fair?
   OR
   Help organize and run the craft fair?

❖ Write a book for children?
   OR
   Illustrate a children's book with your art?

❖ Write a graphic novel?
   OR
   A book of poetry?

❖ Take a class in calligraphy?
   OR
   Origami?

❖ Own an electric bicycle?
   OR
   A dirt bike?

❖ Go with your family to the next Summer Olympics?
   OR
   The next Winter Olympics?

❖ Go to a rodeo?
   OR
   A powwow?

❖ Go shopping at a big city mall?
   OR
   Go to see a Broadway musical at a theatre?

❖ Take a back-stage tour at that theatre?
   OR
   Get invited to meet the actors?

❖ See the next total eclipse of the sun?
OR
See a rare wild animal?

❖ Teach a dog some new tricks?
OR
Take lessons in dog grooming?

❖ Learn how to draw people?
OR
How to draw animals?

❖ Learn how to draw flowers and plants?
OR
How to draw buildings?

❖ Play Monopoly?
OR
Chess?

❖ Play Scrabble?
OR
Truth or Dare?

❖ Learn how to play Bridge?
OR
Poker?

❖ Play horseshoes?
OR
Tennis?

❖ Play pickleball?
OR
Pool?

❖ Play beach volleyball?
OR
Beach badminton?

❖ Play golf?
OR
Shuffleboard?

❖ Play mini-golf?
OR
Pick-up basketball?

❖ Play baseball?
OR
Watch the game and cheer?

❖ Play street hockey?
OR
Ice hockey at an arena?

❖ Spend a day at a waterpark?
OR
Go ziplining?

❖ Go bungee jumping off the top of a mountain?
OR
Kitesurfing?

❖ Go beachcombing?
   OR
   Metal-detecting for buried treasure?

❖ Send a message in a bottle?
   OR
   Find one?

❖ Take piano lessons?
   OR
   Saxophone lessons?

❖ All your clothes accidentally get dyed hot pink?
   OR
   Mud brown?

❖ A glass of lemonade?
   OR
   Iced tea?

❖ Have long hair you wear in braids?
   OR
   A bun?

❖ Play lawn croquet?
   OR
   Lawn bowling?

❖ Learn how to be a better photographer?
   OR
   Take a ceramics course?

❖ Visit Iceland in summer?
OR
Alaska?

❖ Learn how to make a chair?
OR
A lamp?

❖ Take a flight in an ultra-light plane?
OR
A glider?

❖ Take a boxing lesson?
OR
Rope climbing?

❖ Try out yoga?
OR
Playing the bagpipes?

❖ Learn how to play the pennywhistle?
OR
Harmonica?

❖ Take a lesson in Irish dancing?
OR
Sumo wrestling?

❖ Spend all day in your pajamas?
OR
Your bathing suit?

❖ All your shoes are accidentally covered in permanent glitter?
OR
Seashells?

❖ Teach someone younger than you how to do something?
OR
Teach someone older than you how to do something?

❖ Stay up really late?
OR
Get up really early?

❖ Dance?
Or
Sing?

❖ Play darts?
OR
Ping-pong?

❖ Take classes in woodcarving?
OR
Classes in sculpture?

❖ Join volunteers helping to put out summer wildfires?
OR
Help people escape the wildfires?

❖ Take a class in macrame?
 OR
 Embroidery?

❖ Learn how to use a potter's wheel?
 OR
 A knitting machine?

❖ Design costumes for figure skaters to compete in?
 OR
 For Olympian runners to compete in?

❖ Play soccer?
 OR
 American football?

❖ Learn how to make candles?
 OR
 Soap?

❖ Make your own granola?
 OR
 Shampoo?

❖ Go snorkeling on a coral reef?
 OR
 Diving for pearls?

❖ Meet a mermaid?
 OR
 Be a mermaid, for 1 day?

❖ Volunteer at a wildlife rescue center?
OR
At a zoo?

❖ Own a freshwater aquarium?
OR
Saltwater aquarium?

❖ Eat mussels?
OR
Sushi?

❖ Visit the Galapagos Islands?
OR
Tasmania?

❖ Visit Greenland?
OR
Antarctica?

❖ Visit the Florida Keys?
OR
New Mexico?

❖ Learn more about rattlesnakes?
OR
Tarantulas?

❖ Take fencing lessons?
OR
Archery lessons?

❖ Learn how to invest your money?
OR
How to budget your money?

❖ Take classes in gymnastics?
OR
Ballet?

❖ Learn ballroom dancing?
OR
Pole-vaulting?

❖ Learn how to make a soufflé?
OR
Donuts?

❖ Eat fudge?
OR
Salt-water taffy?

❖ Play solitaire?
OR
Checkers?

❖ Take a lesson in mime?
OR
Archery?

❖ Learn how to fly a drone?
OR
How to build and launch rockets?

❖ Be a contestant on a TV game show? What show is it?
OR
Be a contestant on a TV reality show? What show?

❖ Create a new TV game show that's a hit? What is it?
OR
Create a new reality TV show? What is it?

❖ Win a pie-eating contest?
OR
A limbo contest?

❖ Win a speed-walking race?
OR
A swimming race?

❖ Help harvest hay in July?
OR
Grapes in October?

❖ Join the archeological team excavating ancient Pompei, in Italy?
OR
Join paleontologists searching for dinosaur fossils and trackways in Utah?

❖ Meet your favorite actor in a TV show? Who are they?
OR
Your favorite actor in movies? Who?

❖ Help gather honey from beehives?
OR
Gather eggs from chickens?

❖ Make and fly a model airplane?
OR
A kite?

❖ Pick oranges?
OR
Apples?

❖ Your family buys a hot tub?
OR
An above-ground pool?

❖ Move around the room at a party and talk to everyone?
OR
Just have a few longer conversations with people you already know?

❖ Order the same food everyone else is getting at a fine dining restaurant?
OR
Suggest everyone get what you're having?

❖ You invent a new flavor of toothpaste that everyone likes?
OR
A new kind of pizza that's really popular?

❖ You go for a week's vacation to a 5-star hotel on Cape Cod in Massachusetts?
OR
A 3-star hotel near Cape Canaveral in Florida?

❖ You take a city vacation to Boston?
OR
Austin, Texas?

❖ Be a guest at a garden wedding this summer?
OR
At a more formal wedding, held indoors?

❖ Get to do anything you feel like doing all summer this year?
OR
Get to do anything you feel like doing every Friday afternoon for the rest of this year?

❖ Live in Paris, France for 1 year?
OR
Live in London, England for 1 year?

❖ Keep your birthday on the same day it is now?
OR
Change to a different day, maybe in a different month? What day and month would you choose?

❖ Have a hobby of entering contests?
OR
Collecting rare coins?

❖ Live in a house that has no electricity?
  OR
  That has no bathtub or shower?

❖ Live in a house where you can't see any of your neighbors' houses?
  OR
  Live in a house that is almost touching the neighbors' houses?

❖ Be a prince or princess for 1 day?
  OR
  Be a king or queen for 1 day?

❖ You're hired as a special consultant to the engineers who design cars. What changes will you recommend?
  OR
  You're hired as a special consultant to your school district. What changes will you recommend?

❖ Go to lunch with any person you choose who lived in the past? Who are they?
  OR
  Meet someone who will live in the future for your lunch date? Who are they?

❖ You have invented a new kind of restaurant. What kind of food do they serve?
  OR
  You've invented a new kind of fast food. What is it?

❖ Start a hot new trend?
OR
You follow a new trend? What is it?

❖ Go on the TV show Shark Tank to pitch your business idea?
OR
You're one of the 'sharks' on that program?

❖ Help build tiny homes for unhoused people in your city?
OR
Help raise money to build these homes?

❖ Learn how to do 5 card tricks?
OR
5 magic tricks?

❖ Be able to dance on your toes?
OR
Do a perfect cartwheel?

❖ Invent a new cartoon character, like Bullwinkle?
OR
Invent a new comic book character, like Archie?

❖ You invent a major improvement to computers. What is it?
OR
You invent a major improvement to phones. What is it?

❖ You invent a new game. What is it?
OR
You invent a new sport. What is it?

❖ You invent a new toy for kids. What is it?
OR
You invent a new game that people your age like. What is it?

❖ You invent a new hairstyle. It can be for males, or females, or unisex. Describe it.
OR
You invent a new item of clothing. It could be to wear to school or work, or it could be casual or streetwear. What is it?

❖ You invent a new style of bathing suit. What is it and who do you think will like it?
OR
You invent a new style of jeans. What's different about them from all the jean styles that are already available?

❖ You invent a new safety rule for your school or workplace. What is it?
OR
You invent a new rule for your family. What is it?

❖ Live in a haunted castle?
OR
Where you live now?

❖ Invent a new movie supervillain? Who are they and what's so terrible about them?
OR
Invent a new movie heroine or hero? Who are they, and what's so good about them?

❖ You invent a new kind of school and you get to be a pupil there?
OR
The principal?

❖ You suddenly discover that your best friend is secretly an alien from a distant planet?
OR
Suddenly discover that you are actually an alien? Your home planet is millions of light-years away.

❖ Invent a new cryptocurrency? Why is it better than Bitcoin and other cryptos that already exist?
OR
You are the person whose job it is to sell this new cryptocurrency. How will you do this?

❖ Would you rather visit family members who live far away by taking a train to get to where they live?
OR
Take an airplane, to get there faster?

❖ Switch to using wind power?
OR
Solar power?

❖ Invent a new kind of salty snack food?
OR
A new kind of sugary candy?

❖ Have a personal driver who takes you everywhere you want to go?
OR
Have a personal helper who always does all your schoolwork or, if you have a job, they always do all the job tasks you don't enjoy?

❖ Be a plant explorer in the Amazon, searching for plants that might help humanity?
OR
Be an animal explorer, searching the world for undiscovered species of animals?

❖ Be rich?
OR
Be famous?

❖ Meet a tribe of people who have never met other humans before?
OR
Meet the last Neanderthal people on earth, who have somehow survived for many thousands of years since we thought they went extinct?

❖ Invent a new musical instrument? What is it?
OR
Invent a new tool? What is it?

❖ Choose a name for a new color of nail polish? What is it?
OR
Choose a name for a new model of car? What is it?

❖ Open your own store? What kind of store is it? What does it sell?
OR
Open your own restaurant? What kind of restaurant? What kind of food does it offer?

❖ Save up for something big you want to buy? What is it?
OR
Spend on smaller things you want when you want them?

❖ Give parents some pointers on how to understand their kids?
OR
Give kids useful information on understanding their parents?

❖ Be a guest on a popular podcast?
OR
On a radio show?

❖ Have one magic ability? What is it?
OR
Be able to give one magic ability to anyone you choose?

❖ Be 10 years older than you are today? Why?
OR
10 years younger?

❖ Use a gift card to buy one big thing?
OR
5 smaller things?

❖ Live in a place where everyone always knows when it's going to rain or snow next?
OR
Never know when it's going to rain or snow?

❖ Live your life backwards, so you get younger and younger until finally you are a new baby?
OR
Live your life forwards, until finally you are a very old person?

❖ Have to spend all of next year being a student in grade 2?
OR
Grade 8?

❖ Live next door to a family with 26 children?
OR
26 cats?

❖ Find out that the family next door are witches?
OR
Fae?

❖ Find out that the family next door are dragon shifters?
   OR
   Werewolves?

❖ Have a beautiful lawn all around your house?
   OR
   A meadow filled with flowers?

❖ That summer never ends?
   OR
   The best day of your life never ends?

❖ That you never have to get up to an alarm and can sleep as late as you want every day?
   OR
   You never have to go to bed until you feel like it?

❖ Join a group to play Dungeons and Dragons once a week?
   OR
   Get together to play Kids on Bikes?

❖ Join an annual wildlife bird count?
   OR
   A local citizen science project?

❖ Plan a fun summer full of activities for a child?
   OR
   Someone else plans a full summer vacation of activities for you?

❖ Have to take 1 huge pill once a day?
OR
10 small pills once a day?

❖ Have to wear an orthopedic boot for 6 weeks this summer because you broke your ankle BUT you get to laze around a lot?
OR
Have to wear an arm cast for 12 weeks after a fracture AND you can do almost everything you usually do?

❖ Spend your summer at a rented lakeside cottage?
OR
At your own tiny cabin in the woods?

❖ Get to live for 1 hour as a spider?
OR
A fly?

❖ Spend your entire summer vacation living in another country? Where?
OR
In a part of your own country that you've never been to? Where?

❖ Have a job, or go to a school where you can wear anything you want?
OR
There's a uniform and it's a plain tee shirt and jeans. That's what everyone wears, every day.

❖ Never, ever in your life have to eat soup again?
OR
Take vitamins?

❖ Never, ever in your life be confused?
OR
Lost?

❖ Live in a home where every wall is painted orange?
OR
Black?

❖ Enter a log-splitting contest?
OR
Go to a lumberjack festival?

❖ Eat barbequed rattlesnake at a festival?
OR
A monkey brain sandwich?

❖ Sample gator tails in Florida?
OR
A pickle dog at the Minnesota State Fair?

❖ Have cucumber sandwiches for lunch?
OR
Cold chicken salad?

❖ Time travel back to relive your favorite summer?
OR
Make this summer the best one of your life?

In this book...

You've thought about who you are, what you like and what you want – or don't want.

And you've asked friends and family members some of these questions, too.

You can go back through this book any time, or many times. Maybe your answers will change!

Thinking about and answering these questions helps you know a lot more about who you are, what you value and what YOU want for your summer and your life. And that's always the first step in getting the most joy in your life!

Listening to the answers of others is also important. It helps you know and understand them better.

And here's your next challenge! Have fun writing your own Would You Rather questions for family and friends!

How many can you think of?

How will you answer?

Have fun with it...

And thanks for reading!

Jesse

Here are all the titles in this new FUN ACTIVITIES AND JOKES FOR KIDS series, all available where you bought this book:

❖ **Would You Rather Word Game For Smart Kids** -- 725+ Fun and Challenging Would You Rather Questions For Kids and Families.

❖ **Summer Would You Rather Game Book** -- 260+ Fun and Challenging Would You Rather Questions For Kids, Tweens, Teens and Families.

❖ **Knock Knock Jokes For Children** -- 500+ Fun Knock Knock Jokes For Kids.

❖ **Jokes For Kids** -- 550+ Laugh-Out-Loud Jokes and Riddles For Kids and Families.

❖ **Smelly Funny Facts Book for Kids 9-12** – Humor to Get Kids Reading and Laughing

And for teachers:

❖ **What's So Funny?** – A Teaching Resource For Grades 3 to 6

Find out more at: www.CrimsonHillBooks.com

Discover MORE about your favorite pets and animals in these books:

- I Want A Dog
- I Want A Cat
- I Want A Bearded Dragon
- I Want A Leopard Gecko
- Fun Leopard Gecko and Bearded Dragon Facts for Kids
- Fun Reptile Facts for Kids
- Fun Dog Facts for Kids
- Fun Cat Facts for Kids
- Fun Pony Facts for Kids
- Fun Horse Facts for Kids
- Fun Bird Facts for Kids
- Fun Backyard Bird Facts for Kids
- Fun Dinosaur Facts for Kids
- Fun T-Rex Facts for Kids
- Fun Bug Facts for Kids
- Fun Snake Facts for Kids
- Fun Spider Facts for Kids

You can find ALL the books in the Fun Animal Facts For Kids series at: www.CrimsonHillBooks.com